Poppy Cotton is an ordinary girl
who lives in a pretty little cottage with
her mum and dad and the baby twins,
Angel and Archie. When she is good
everybody calls her Princess Poppy.
Her grandpa says that every
little girl is a princess, especially
when she is kind and helpful.
Are you kind and helpful too?

Honeypot Hill

Can you find the places that
Poppy visits in this story?

Saffron Thimble's
Sewing Shop

To the City

The Orchards

Paddle Steamer
Quay

Aun
Marigo
Gene
Stor

Lavender Valley
Garden Centre

Healing House and Garden

The Worthington's House

Melody
Maker's Music
Shop

Lavender Lake

Lavender Lake
School of Dance

Bumble Bee's
Teashop

Peppermint
Pond

Hedgerows Hotel
where Mimosa lives

SCHOOL

Rosehip School

Summer Meadow

Christmas Corner

Wildspice Woods

Honeysuckle
Cottage
Poppy's House

Forget-Me-Not Cottage
Grandpa's House and Office

Poppy
Field

Cornsilk Castle
and Courtyard

oneypot Cottage
and Granny Bumble's House

Blossom
Bakehouse

Village Hall

Sage's
Vet Surgery

Post Office

Beehive
Beauty Salon

Barley Farm
The Meadowsweets' House

Riverside
Stables

River Swan

Honeypot Hill
Railway Station

To Camomile Cove
via Periwinkle Lane

N
W — E
S

Visit Princess Poppy for fun, games,
puzzles, activities and lots more at
www.princesspoppy.com

THE ROYAL PARADE
A RED FOX BOOK 978 0 552 57026 8

First published in Great Britain by Picture Corgi,
an imprint of Random House Children's Publishers UK
A Random House Group Company

This Red Fox edition published in 2013

1 3 5 7 9 10 8 6 4 2

Text copyright © Janey Louise Jones, 2012
Illustrations copyright © Picture Corgi Books, 2012
Illustrations by Veronica Vasylenko

The right of Janey Louise Jones and Veronica Vasylenko to be identified as the author and illustrator
of this work has been asserted in accordance with the Copyright, Designs and Patents Act 1988.

Red Fox Books are published by Random House Children's Publishers UK,
61–63 Uxbridge Road, London W5 5SA

www.randomhousechildrens.co.uk
www.randomhouse.co.uk
www.princesspoppy.com
Addresses for companies within The Random House Group Limited can be found at:
www.randomhouse.co.uk/offices.htm
THE RANDOM HOUSE GROUP Limited Reg. No. 954009
A CIP catalogue record for this book is available from the British Library.

Printed in China

Princess Poppy

The Royal Parade

Written by Janey Louise Jones

RED FOX

*Especially for (Princess) Elfie (Gleeson),
who loves to dress up, just like Princess Poppy*

The Royal Parade

featuring

Mum

Honey

Princess Poppy

Saffron

David
(The village vet)

Farmer Meadowsweet

Granny Bumble
(Honey's granny)

The Honeypot Hill dress-up parade and street party was a week away. This year the theme was royalty.

"I am going to dress up as a royal princess," said Poppy as she looked through the dressing-up box in the attic.

"I am going to be a queen," said Honey.

They carried a bundle of dressing-up
clothes down to Poppy's bedroom to have
a better look.

Honey chose a
golden dress fit
for a queen

and Poppy
settled on a red
princess dress.

Both were gorgeous but rather shabby.
"Let's ask Saffron to help us mend
them," said Poppy.

"Where are you two going?" asked Mum.
"Aren't you coming to the Village Hall?
Granny Bumble is giving out jobs for
the parade."

Poppy was so excited about her costume
that she had forgotten.

When they arrived at the hall it was packed.
Everyone wanted to help.

Granny Bumble read out her list.

There was a lot to do. But Poppy was not down for anything.

She was very disappointed.

Bumble Bee's Teashop

Granny Bumble's party List

Sandwiches   Mrs Turner and Sweetpea

Drinks   Lavender and Marigold

Cakes   Honey and Me

Tables and Chairs   Grandpa

Music   Mr + Mrs Melody + Abigail

Decorations   Saffron

Honeypot Hill Olympics   David

Parade Cart   Farmer Meadowsweet

Medals for races   Holly Mallow

"I need help with the parade cart," said Farmer Meadowsweet.

"I'll do it!" Poppy said.

"Grand!" he replied. "It will need cleaning and decorating. You can do that and I will get Hermione, my old cart horse, ready."

Poppy was thrilled to have such an important job. The cart led the parade every year.

That night it took Poppy ages to get to sleep. Her dreams were filled with thoughts of the parade.

The next day she felt very tired so she decided to take things easy.

Poppy did not go to Barley Farm.

On Monday morning Poppy and Honey
went to Saffron's Sewing Shop with
their dresses.

They chose
new sequins
and ribbons,

and picked out
some crowns.

Then Saffron
pinned up
their hems.

After a while Saffron explained that she had to make the bunting for the parade. She promised she would finish their costumes later in the week.

"Oh, that reminds me," said Poppy. "I must wash the cart."

She thanked Saffron, said goodbye to Honey and went off towards Barley Farm.

As Poppy walked through the village, day-
dreaming about her costume, she bumped
into David. He was going to mark out the
tracks for the Honeypot Hill Olympics.

"Can I help?" said Poppy. She decided
she would go to the farm later.

"Of course," replied David.

Poppy did not make it to Barley Farm
that day either.

On Tuesday Poppy set off for the farm nice and early. She met Saffron on the way.

"Hi, Poppy," Saffron called. "I have almost finished your costume. Would you like to come and have a look?"

"Oh, yes please!" Poppy replied.

She would wash the cart straight afterwards, she decided.

The village bustled with activity and the week flashed by.

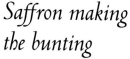

Saffron making the bunting

Mum and Aunt Marigold squeezing lemons for the lemonade

Honey and her granny baking cakes

The Melody family rehearsing the music

On Saturday morning Poppy woke up with a start. The phone was ringing.

It was the day of the parade. But she did not feel excited. She felt worried.

"That was Farmer Meadowsweet!" said Mum. "He is not happy. He wants you to go to the farm. Now."

Mum was right. Farmer Meadowsweet was
not happy and Poppy knew why. She *had*
meant to do her job but other things had
got in the way.

"We will have to cancel the parade," said
the farmer crossly.

"I'm sorry," said Poppy. "I did mean to
do it but there was so much other stuff
happening. I will do it now."

Farmer Meadowsweet tutted doubtfully,
quite sure it would not be ready in time.

The farmer was angry and disappointed but he saw how sorry Poppy was and how much she wanted to fix things. He offered to help her.

Poppy worked very hard. She was determined not to ruin the parade.

But they were running out of time.

At two o'clock the parade began.

Poppy and her friends, dressed in their royal finery, stood in the beautifully decorated cart as Hermione pulled it through Honeypot Hill.

There was clapping and cheering, tooting
and hooting, music, balloons, bunting
and streamers.

When the parade ended it was time for
the street party!

Poppy ran over to help.

She finished
setting the tables,

laid out the
sandwiches,

put a cupcake
at each place

and poured
the lemonade.

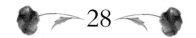

Everyone tucked in.
It was delicious!

After tea the Honeypot Hill
Olympics began.

The egg-and-spoon race
was funny, the three-legged
race was hilarious, and
throwing the beanbag in
the hoop was a giggle!
But the best thing of
all was that Poppy
was chosen to give
out the prizes!

"Poppy, you were a very helpful Parade Princess in the end!" chuckled Farmer Meadowsweet when the races were over. "That truly was a grand parade!"

Poppy smiled and promised herself that she would never let things get in the way like that again.